WHO EVER HEARD OF A JEWISH MISSIONARY?

A Jew for Jesus Tells His Story

By Bob Mendelsohn

A Purple Pomegranate Book
Purple Pomegranate Productions

Who Ever Heard of a Jewish Missionary?
by Bob Mendelsohn
© Copyright 1999 by Purple Pomegranate Productions

Cover design by Daniela Koger Meyer

All rights reserved. Nothing in this book shall be reprinted or reproduced, electronically or in any other manner, without express written permission. For more information, write to:

Reprint Permission
Purple Pomegranate Productions
84 Page Street, San Francisco, CA 94102

Published by

JEWS F✡R JESUS®
60 Haight Street
San Francisco, CA 94102
USA

JEWS F✡R JESUS®
P.O. Box 925
Sydney NSW 2001
Australia

ISBN 10: 1-881022-43-9
ISBN 13: 978-1-881022-43-5

WHO EVER HEARD OF A JEWISH MISSIONARY?

I don't think I had ever been so nervous. My mouth was terribly dry, yet the palms of my hands were puddled with sweat. I had studied intensely for a whole year to prepare me for these next few hours. Would I stumble over the Hebrew I had studied so carefully? Would I remember my speech, the only part of my *bar mitzvah* I was to present in English?

I was about to become a "son of the commandment" through the ceremony that initiates a thirteen-year-old boy into the religious life of the Jewish community! I would be responsible to obey the Torah and all its accompanying codes of oral tradition. Quite a heavy responsibility for one who, in many ways, was still a child.

The rabbi called me forward to lead the *shacharit*, the morning service. I faced a frightening sea of faces. I imagined each person with a clipboard, waiting to evaluate my performance and turn in a score to some panel of judges. Not that there were any such clipboards or judges, but I was greatly concerned with doing well to please and impress everyone who had come to hear me.

Latecomers trickled in and the 1,000-seat sanctuary was filling up quickly. Reassuring smiles of friends and relatives helped. Even my Spanish teacher from school was there, along with the third-baseman for the Kansas City Athletics.

It was time to start. After a few minutes of canting the familiar melodies, my nervousness dissolved.

The Torah scroll, in its beautiful velvet cover, was removed from the ark. I led the congregation in the *Sh'ma*, "Hear, O Israel, the LORD our God, the LORD is one." I reverently carried the Torah around the sanctuary for all the people to see and kiss.

Back on the *bimah*, my Torah reading went well. I felt happy to have some of my relatives up there with me, especially when it was my father's turn to recite one of the seven benedictions. I relaxed a bit more as I sang my Scripture portions; I chanted the *musaf* for the Sabbath. Then it was over and I sat down.

Afterwards, there was plenty of food and drink and merry-making. People congratulated me and wished me great success in the future. I felt good. It was over and I had done well; I could relax and enjoy being the guest of honor.

My name is Bob Mendelsohn. I was born on November 4, 1951 in Kansas City, Missouri, at Menorah Hospital.

My father, Elic, was born in Kansas City in 1921. His parents came over from Russia/Poland. Dad grew up to be a salesman—not of one particular item, but of many. He knew how to make people want what he was selling. He sold many products: stuffed toys, Papercraft Paper, or Niles and Moser Cigars—even Nelson Bibles for a time.

My mother, Helen (*née*) Wolf, was born in 1922 in Kansas City. She and my father met on Yom Kippur in 1937. It was downstairs in the social hall of the synagogue, during services. My dad struck up a conversation with her using a line that could have been right out of a Gene Kelly movie. He snapped his fingers near her face, she turned, and he said, "Thanks. I wanted to see the face that went with those legs." Dad was Orthodox and Mom usually attended a Reform temple. However, to honor the family on the High Holidays, she and her mother always went to the Orthodox *shul* along with Mom's maternal grandmother. They all sat upstairs with the other women, but now and then, my mother went downstairs where the teens socialized.

Mom and Dad married in June, 1942. Dad served in the Navy in World War II. He was in Pearl Harbor on

December 7, 1941 on the USS Wharton, rescuing women and children and delivering them to safety after the attack. Later he served in Europe (Italy, Southern France) and Northern Africa, as well as Alaska and the islands of Macon and Tarawa. Finally, in 1945 he was stationed in Norfolk, Virginia, which is where he and my mother were living when my brother Michael was born that same year.

Michael is a salesman too; he worked with my dad for years. Now he is an interior decorator in Kansas City. My sister Judy, born in 1948, also lives in KC and sells advertising for various newspapers. She also works at the Welcome Center at Hallmark Cards.

I'm the baby, born in 1951. And I am a missionary. So how did that happen? After all, I always took my Judaism very seriously.

Being Jewish was always a fact of life for me. My mother worked at the synagogue in the office, taught kindergarten in the Sunday school, coached our synagogue youth group's musicals and dramas and was president of the Marcella Rodin Auxilliary for volunteers.

Attending synagogue, celebrating holidays at home—this was the norm as far back as I can remember. I bowled with Jewish kids, played basketball with Jewish friends and learned about our people in Hebrew school. I never questioned my Jewish identity. The culinary side of that identity was nurtured by regular visits to both our grandmothers' houses. My dad's mom, Bubbe, used to make her own ground horseradish and pickles—the latter she kept in brine out on her porch. Bubbe also made delicious apple strudel. My mother's mom, Grandma Bessie, was not so "old world" but still, she was definitively Jewish. I don't remember her cooking so many traditional dishes, but she loved to feed us and always brought banana cream pies to family dinners.

But being Jewish was more than a familial identity for me. It was a calling.

Whereas some boys tolerated Hebrew school, I was devout. Part of my devotion, I suppose, was due to the fact that I could excel. Cognitive learning (handling facts/figures) always came easily to me. Much of Hebrew school was a test of cognitive skills, so I did well. Doing well mattered to me, and in Judaism I found my niche. Encouragement from the rabbis was also key. I wanted their approval and they bestowed it generously.

I was recognized as a spiritual leader in my youth group and during the afternoons, when I went to Hebrew school, I led the *Minchah* and *Ma'ariv* services.

I was bar mitzvah in 1964 and finished Hebrew school in 1966. I was very involved in our youth group, SYO (Synagogue Youth Organization). SYO was a Midwest regional subsidiary of the National Conference of Synagogue Youth (NCSY), the Orthodox youth movement. I was the local vice president, editor of our paper and member of the regional planning committee for conferences.

In 1966, the national organization of Boy Scouts was looking for a good Jewish experience to report for their magazine and someone at my synagogue suggested me. I guess I was the all-American Midwestern Jew—the magazine published an article about me with photos, which added to my high profile in our community.

I conducted the morning prayer services on special Shabbats. I *davened* quickly and got better and faster as I grew. When I led the Shabbat services, there would have been upwards of 300 people. Feelings? Pride that I could do so well. Spiritual thoughts? None . . .

My prayers were institutional. Yes, I believed that God was a wonderful Being. I believed he was real because that's what we (Jewish people) believe. That was all I knew. God was not knowable. He was not personal. He just was. I gave up talking to God early on, having noticed that the few prayers I offered up never came to pass. Maybe, I thought,

God had not answered in a personal way because so many people were talking to him about so much all the time. Maybe he took our prayers under advisement. In any case, I grew up with the motto, *Qué será, será*, what will be will be, and don't expect God to do much about it. Though I didn't talk much to God, I did talk with others about him—and concluded that God was big and important and well, Other. And there was something of that mystique to the religion of Judaism.

Even though I was officially a "son of the commandment" (the Law) at thirteen, it was not until three years later that I became more serious about observing it.

It was summer. I went to youth camp in Wild Rose, Wisconsin and there encountered Jimmy. He was a man from New York City, a *baal teshuva* who came to work as a volunteer at Camp Moshava. He confronted me with my compromises and challenged me to live a more orthopractic life. I had always been proud to be Jewish. There was some mystique to all these dos and don'ts that were supposed to improve me as a person and, in particular, as a Jew. The fact that my parents were less observant than I felt they should have been made it all the more attractive. Sixteen-year-olds generally feel they know more than their parents, and here was an opportunity for me to be different from them and have something of my own while intensifying something that had always been important to me—my Jewishness. So I returned from camp very enthused about my religion.

I was fervent, not so much about God, but about "doing" Judaism correctly. Indirectly, my observance was connected to God since I was fairly certain that he existed, and that he had commanded us Jews to do certain *mitzvot*. It was my job, as a Jew, to observe these commands and comply. I figured that even if there were no God, it couldn't hurt to comply. And because compromise was a very bad word in my youthful understandings, and because I saw only absolutes, I stopped eating out with my parents and stopped attending their synagogue. I couldn't eat kosher food at home and non-kosher food when we went out. I couldn't drive to synagogue and park a block away and pretend to walk. I walked all the way to a different, closer synagogue, *Ohev Yisrael*. As far as I was concerned, my devotion had to be 100%—or nothing.

When I went to university (Washington University in St. Louis), I found a way to continue my Jewish education: I gave a rabbi's son guitar lessons in exchange for lessons in religion from his father. I enjoyed persuading others to be more *frum* as well, bringing friends with me to learn from the rabbi. Several of us laid *tefillin* each morning.

My concept of God didn't change, but my understanding of his demands on our lives did. God still was big and other, but now I felt like I was keeping more of the rules. Observance tends to make one feel holier.

Yet hard as I tried, I always seemed to fall short; there was always something more to do, or not do. My efforts never seemed good enough. There was always something missing in my efforts to please God. He seemed so insatiable. The road to being a good Jew was very long and seemed to be lined with more books than the shelves at the 42nd Street Library could hold. The *ruach* (spirit) we longed to experience in the songfests was never quite enough to fill us (although it did exhaust us). Nothing was ever enough. There was always more learning, more *kavanah* (devotion), more attention to minutiae, more people to bring in, more kindnesses to extend, more stories to memorize.

One Friday night, I had an experience that may seem silly or small but it was the beginning of a great change. I had attended the erev Shabbat services at *Tiferes Israel Chevra Kadisha* in suburban St. Louis. The rabbi had been teaching me personally for months. It was an enjoyable night with good conversation and personal attention from the rabbi. But when I came home, I had a problem. My *Shabbes goy* (the gentile who took care of details I couldn't attend to during the 25 hours of Sabbath—like turning my lights on and off) was gone. He had left for a party—and had left me in the proverbial lurch. There I was in Eliot Hall, the men's high rise (which has long since gone co-ed), and the bright overhead light was shining in my face as I lay down for the night. I said my prayers. I almost asked God to bring along Rick or even Mike or Chuck or one of the other Jewish students in our dorm who were not as observant and might have turned off the light for me. But I didn't ask, and as a religious Jew I could not ignite or shut it off according to the rabbinic interpretation of the Scripture. What a dilemma. What was I to do?

After about 30 minutes of arguing with God "Tevye-style" (remember *Fiddler on the Roof*?), I got up and shut off the light. I felt horrible. I'd just broken a commandment—on purpose! How could I go to synagogue the next day without feeling like a hypocrite?

I didn't go back to services the next morning; I felt too guilty. The rabbi called a few days later to inquire after me. I told him some things were changing and I wouldn't be back for a while. He didn't know my shame. I couldn't disclose these things to him. What would he think of me if I did?

My disillusionment with myself eventually evolved into a disillusionment with "the system." School and religion—arenas which had once been a source for much of my self esteem—lost their luster.

I dropped out of university in December 1970. I became a hippie and a wandering Jew, hoping to find some peace and meaning for my life. I hitchhiked to New Orleans, Louisiana and on to Atlanta, Georgia. I stayed at Emory University with some people I had met on the streets. Before long I "fell in love" and moved in with a woman seven years my senior. We used to attend the Unitarian church on Sunday mornings. She was open-minded and I just wanted to be with her. I found the church dull, but not offensive to me as a Jew, since there were no real and absolute statements made about God or other religions.

Then, one Sunday afternoon in February, a group of four well-dressed men approached me on Peachtree Street in Atlanta. They looked foreign with their crewcuts and their white shirts and thin ties. It was 1971 and I was a classic hippie with long hair and beads, no shoes and a tie-dye T-shirt. These men were aliens to me. And their message was just as alien.

They used the expression "turn or burn" as they told me that if I didn't accept Jesus, I would go to hell. I told them that I was Jewish and their religion made no sense to me. I wanted no part of their message. Their words conjured up images of burning bodies during the Holocaust and of White Supremacists burning crosses on the lawns of Jews and Blacks.

I was angry at these men. In fact, I hated them.

It wasn't that I objected to Jesus. I didn't know enough about him to object or not. But I hated people telling me that I needed their religion—that mine was somehow not good enough.

I responded to these four men fiercely, yelling at them, saying that they knew nothing about Jewish people or our problems! Who were they to tell me to join them in eternity—they wanted to convert me to their gentile god? What rubbish! Quit being a Jew? I don't think so. I was loud and raging. I think they got the point. I felt perfectly righteous in my response. Yet other things had pointed out to me that I was in no way righteous.

For example, before going to Atlanta, I spent some time in New Orleans, Louisiana. There, I saw myself for what I was one morning on Bourbon Street. It was about 3 A.M. I had spent the day lying in Jackson Square Park outside of the Catholic cathedral. Occasionally, I picked up my twelve-string guitar and strummed popular tunes like "Suite: Judy Blue Eyes" from Crosby, Stills and Nash and "Knights in White Satin" from the Moody Blues. Crowds gathered and sang along. It was like a Southern love-in. What a time! That night, a group of us began to dance on the streets outside a jazz-filled nightclub. We were all in a chain, dancing our way down the narrow street weaving our way through the tourists and the hawkers. I felt so full of peace and love and happiness. Then I looked to my right and saw a man standing next to me—and I despised him. It was unreasonable. I didn't know him, except to observe that his skin was a different color than mine, he was missing a pair of front teeth and he was sweaty. I was ashamed of how I felt. Here I was, supposedly a man of peace and love, yet I didn't love this man. I knew it was wrong but I had no control over my feelings. I simply hated him. I knew that he didn't deserve it—and I knew that I was a hypocrite.

Two weeks later, I was newly arrived in Atlanta and looking for a place to sleep. I heard about a crash pad and I went to stay there. While a fellow traveler was in the showers cleaning up from his day, I rifled his trousers looking for cash. Sure enough, I found $5 and took it, pocketing it while no one looked. The guilt was horrible inside me, but what was I to do? I was hungry; I had been panhandling, begging, and here was an easy five-spot. I knew that it was wrong, but again I felt unable to do otherwise. Where could I turn? I went to Washington, D.C. and marched for peace, but I knew . . . I was not truly a man of peace. I was a person who could hate people I didn't know. I was a person who could steal.

Within the year, I returned to Kansas. I had taken a beating, mentally and emotionally. I had not found the answers I thought would be forthcoming from my wandering hippie lifestyle. My father bought me a one-way ticket from Washington, D.C. so that I could celebrate Passover with the family.

We began the seder but when we started to read the *Haggadah* I interrupted. "Are we going to do the same thing that we do every year?" No one was prepared for that. "What do you mean?" they wanted to know.

"It's just that every year we say the same words—but do we know what we are saying? Can't we just talk through the seder tonight?" I asked. My mother was very keen to see some changes anyway, so she stood up and said, "I have an idea. Let's have Robert lead the seder tonight!" Normally my parents (and most others) call me Bob. "Robert" was used only if I was in trouble or about to be honored. I didn't know if I was in trouble or not, but my father agreed to my mother's proposal. We began to celebrate the seder and to interpret the exodus from Egypt in light of the civil rights movement and the need for all people to be free. We followed the Haggadah loosely, but we didn't rely on the text as we moved through the celebration.

We reached the part of the Haggadah that reads, "Let us sing unto the Lord a new song, praise ye the Lord, Hallelujah."

"What song do we sing now?" my mother wanted to know. I was well aware of the melody and the words we would traditionally sing at that point, but instead, I suggested, "Let's really sing a new song." My sister Judy and cousin Janet began to sing a popular rock and roll song about Jeremiah (not the prophet, but the bullfrog) by a group called "Three Dog Night." The song, ("Joy to the World") was a fun song for teens, but it had nothing to do with the exodus or the spirit of the evening. I said, "No, let's sing something else." However, my sister and cousin—enamored with the freedom of the evening—continued to sing. My other cousin, Nancy, and I began singing "Hallelujah," the chorus from Handel's oratorio *Messiah*.

Imagine the cacophony! Bullfrogs and omnipotence! One grandmother wondered loudly what was going on while the other yelled at my mother to make us stop. When the noise level rose to the breaking point my father yelled, "*Shah!*" The room was hushed. Everyone looked at my father. He picked up the Haggadah and began to read at the point we had stopped. I pushed back from the table, announcing, "That was my fourth cup," and left.

Outside I wondered, "What do I do now?" No one ever left the seder early. At least not in my household. The moon was full. I looked up to heaven. I'd rarely spoken to God in English before. Not much beyond, "Now I lay me down to sleep," when I was a young boy. That night was different. I looked up and said, "Sir. Here I am, trying to bring meaning and relevance to the seder. I'm trying to make it ours. But those people in there (my family) are hypocrites. They don't even believe in you (that was actually not true) and they don't care about anything but getting to page 28 (when we eat). Here I am, trying to do it right and they are still in there going through the motions. *Is there another way?*" I had more to say, but that was the gist of my prayer. Is there another way?

As I was trying to fit the pieces of my life back together, I met a woman named Marva who was doing the same. Marva had been raised in a Christian home but had recently had some kind of personal and intense experience with Jesus. She wanted to tell me about it. Since her thoughts about Jesus included thoughts about me, I tolerated what she had to say.

A month later, I was walking in Kansas City near the Volker Park, home of the Nelson Art Gallery. It is a pristine site in the historic Country Club Plaza. In 1971, it was a gathering place for hippies who congregated there each Sunday afternoon, listening to rock music and tossing Frisbees.

As I passed two people in their late teens, they cried out,

*Elic and Helen Mendelsohn
Spring 1949*

Bob's bar mitzvah 1964

Bob with Elic and Helen at his Hebrew School Graduation 1966

Twenty years of age

*Mr. and Mrs. Bob and Patty Mendelsohn
1977*

High School Graduation

Bob's early years with Jews for Jesus

Sharing his faith in Washington, D.C.

And in San Francisco, too

Telling New York City about Y'shua 1997

Celebrating the bar mitzvah of his son Nathaniel

Grandma Bessie Wolf with her two daughers Pauline and Helen

Bubbe Mary Mendelsohn

Bob and Patty Mendelsohn, now in Australia

"Do you know the Lord is with you?" Oy, I thought. More of those "Jesus people." Like the ones in Atlanta. But strangely, I stopped, asking myself, "Why do I always walk past those people?" I turned around and walked back to them with a challenge. "I'm Jewish; go ahead." I knew they wanted to convert me to their blond-haired, blue-eyed god. I'd seen the movies.

They flipped open their Bibles and began telling me about Jesus right out of the book. They answered some of my questions but were stumped by others. When I asked them about peace on the earth, they answered that they had peace. Personally! They said that when I accepted Jesus, the sky would be bluer and the grass would be greener! Their experience of Christianity was alive and they wanted me to experience it, too. This was so different from my experience in Atlanta. These enthusiastic people had something that they wanted to share with me. And since (unlike Marva), I had no particular interest in them personally, I found myself curious about what they were saying.

Still, I was Jewish and it was my duty to refute these nice people and their nice religion. It was not new for me to discuss religion in this way. Jimmy, the *baal teshuva* from summer camp had given me a book. The title was something like *Missionaries at the Door*, and it provided responses to those who might try to convert Jews to Christianity. I had read that book. These two young people were out of their league and I won the Bible battle. But they won a bigger battle, and so I continued thinking about Jesus.

They won me with their humility. They admitted they did not have all the answers. I'd never heard of religious people not having all the answers—or at least openly admitting they didn't. Every religious person I'd ever met seemed fairly confident in his or her own ability to answer any objection and query. Here were two Christians, ministers I thought, who admitted what they didn't know. Nor did they seem flustered or upset to have to do so. That was very refreshing. Their confidence in the answers they did offer was not based on who they were, but in the One of whom they spoke.

They pointed me to the Source. They urged me to go talk to God and to ask him for answers that they could not provide. That was new. If you wanted to know anything in Orthodox Judaism, you would go to the Talmud or to a rabbi. You would read a book. Ask God? Not likely! He was too busy. And besides, I wasn't altogether sure that he cared about me. Well, these people were absolutely convinced that he did, and that I should be in touch with him about Jesus.

After that encounter, I wanted to talk to Marva again. Whatever interest I may have had in her was eclipsed by the challenge I had decided to take: to find out about Jesus for myself.

It was Friday. We stayed up that entire night reading from the New Testament. We began in the first book, the Gospel of Matthew, and kept reading. We even read parts of the book of the Revelation. How exciting—and a bit scary—to read that apocalyptic book at night!

The part that spoke to me the most was in John, chapter 10. There, Jesus encountered some religious leaders in Jerusalem. He claimed to be the Messiah and equal with God. They picked up stones to stone him and he declared, "For which of my works do you stone me?" That was a stunning statement. I'd read philosophy and anticipated that Jesus the philosopher would say, "For which of my words do you stone me?" But this wasn't a typographical error. This was a religious man, standing in front of other religious leaders, saying something like, "If I've done anything wrong, go ahead and kill me." Wow! Imagine inviting religious people to scrutinize you. It's like asking your mother to tell you if you have any dirt on your trousers after playing outside in the mud. Of course, they'll find the sins.

Now I knew a little something about being inspected by

religious leaders. When I was about fourteen, my mother had knitted a beautiful white sweater with interwoven blue and red cable stitching. How proud I was to wear it to the synagogue one Shabbat. During the course of the service, the rabbi called me to the front and chided me for not dressing suitably (meaning I should have worn a jacket and not a sweater). For added emphasis, he slapped my cheek. Now this was probably not at all typical of most rabbis, but it was my experience and so this is how I thought of religious authorities. How could Jesus have stood in front of such people to invite them to find fault. Even more amazing, these leaders could not find a thing wrong with Jesus!

The person of Jesus was very appealing. The New Testament was a defensible book; the gospel was a defensible story. As I found myself drawn to Jesus I began asking myself, how could I do this? How could I be Jewish and believe in Jesus? It seemed like such a paradox. My upbringing told me that the beliefs that were making so much sense to me were off-limits for a Jew. But what I was reading and what I was sensing from having asked God was this: If Jesus was the Messiah, then the most "right" thing I could do as a Jew, and as a person seeking truth, was to believe. I knew what the consequences would be and did not relish them. It would hurt my family. I would be an outcast. Believing and following Jesus would have a serious impact on my dating life and in fact, on my entire social situation. But, I concluded, if it's the Truth, then that's what I want more than anything. And I continued to read.

My father came into my room on Sunday and saw me pouring over the Bible that Marva had lent me. (I'd hardly stopped reading since Friday night.) "Whose Bible is this?" he asked as he removed it from my hands. "God's," I whispered rather loudly but with a sense of awe. He stormed out of my room, Bible in hand, and tossed it in the kitchen trash. I later retrieved it.

On Monday night, I went to Marva's house. I had concluded from my reading that I did not need "meaning and relevance." I needed and longed for forgiveness.

It was May 1971. I sat on the step of Marva's front porch and prayed with her. I asked God to forgive me, to consider Jesus' atoning death the covering for my sins, to give me a new life. And he did.

I felt an immediate change. I guess it was noticeable because Marva, who wouldn't let me hug her before (she knew my state!) now welcomed me as a brother in Messiah, a fellow disciple. She taught me the song "Amazing Grace" that night. I'd heard Judy Collins sing it before, but didn't understand a thing until that night. It was a joy to sing about grace after truly experiencing it.

That Monday night, I went back to my parents' house in Prairie Village, Kansas, and told them of my new faith. They thought I was crazy. How could a Jew be a Christian? I assured them that my decision was real, that it was based on Truth. My parents were (and are) good people and, in their way, they were very committed Jews; they wanted to do the right thing. My father felt that I should leave the house immediately. My mother convinced him to allow me to spend the night. I went to bed with a sense of real sadness, yet in some inexplicable way, I still had joy in my heart.

I awoke to the sound of yelling. My parents didn't know what to do with me; I didn't know what to do with them. The best solution was for me to move out, which I did that morning. I got a new apartment on Charlotte Street in Kansas City, a new job at Winstead's (an upscale "burger joint"), and most important, I got a new life and a new perspective.

I began to measure reality in terms of God rather than my own self-actualization. Jesus provided the atonement I needed to know God, to relate to him. God was still "other," but he had reached out to his creation—to me—through his Messiah, Jesus.

Before I believed in Jesus, I was discouraged that I

could never measure up. I felt condemned by each and every failure—not because someone was actively chastising me, but because I didn't see any biblical provision of forgiveness for breaking the many rules and regulations.

After I came to faith in Jesus, I was still very much aware of my imperfections, but even more aware of his perfections. He could do what I couldn't—make it through this life without mistakes. He knew the difference between pleasing God and pleasing people. And his ability to please God perfectly—and to die in place of those who deserved God's condemnation—provided atonement, covering for my sin and for anyone else who would claim it. Now that didn't mean I was free to live a life of immorality or hypocrisy, or that I didn't need to concern myself with pleasing God. It meant that I wanted, more than ever, to please this God of forgiveness, this God of love. I could trust him to guide me and when I fell, I could trust him to pick me up.

I didn't run out to become a missionary. But I did begin to preach on the streets immediately, since I wanted others to have this life-saving experience. I went to bars to tell people about Jesus and to Bible studies and churches to learn more about him. I listened to Bible teaching tapes and went to conferences about Jesus. I played songs about Jesus on my twelve-string guitar anywhere and everywhere I could. I truly felt compelled to proclaim God's good love in Jesus.

After about four months, I stuck out my thumb and went hitchhiking again—mostly around Texas, Missouri, Oklahoma and eventually Wichita and Lawrence, Kansas. There I met Steve Churchill, a believer in Jesus who became like a brother to me. We began to pray and ask God how we could serve him in Lawrence.

Steve and I started a church called "The Mustard Seed," a meaningful name to me because Jesus said that is as much faith as we need—the size of a mustard seed. I had learned from experience what God can do with a tiny speck of faith. That's all I had when I realized that if Jesus was true, I wanted to believe. The Mustard Seed church began as a small group of people who wanted to study the Bible together . . . and eventually grew to a community of about 700 people.

I was teaching and pastoring (we didn't use that term . . . it sounded too institutional) when I met Patty, a university freshman who began attending The Mustard Seed. It was 1974. We were married in 1977.

The church was growing by leaps and bounds when I stepped down from my position. I wanted to devote more of myself to finishing university, to my wife and also to my job.

I graduated from the University of Kansas with a Bachelor of Science degree in Education and became a mathematics teacher. I got along well with the students and truly enjoyed my job. I had hoped that this was to be my calling. But there was something else.

I just had to tell people about Jesus—from the very beginning. And so it was inevitable that I would eventually become associated with a group of people who just had to do the same.

I first encountered Jews for Jesus in May of 1973, when their Jewish gospel music group, "The Liberated Wailing Wall," came through Lawrence, Kansas. After meeting them I went out immediately and got a T-shirt made that said, "Jews for Jesus." I liked the way they identified themselves up front. Eight months later, I traveled to California to visit several organizations, including Jews for Jesus.

Moishe Rosen, the founder of Jews for Jesus, was in the office when I came and he invited me to lunch. As we sat in a Chinese restaurant, he asked me something to the effect of, "What can you do to help Jews for Jesus?" I thought it was a pretty good organization and it hadn't occurred to me that I had anything to add. Yet that question riveted me. What can I do to help people find what Jesus offers? How can I use the talents God has given me to serve him today?

I felt a tug, but I had a plan for my life—which at that time did not include being a missionary only to Jewish people. Over the next few years, different people from Jews for Jesus came through the Lawrence area. They generally encouraged me in my efforts to serve God, and usually invited me to join their efforts too.

Finally in 1978, when I was leading a rather predictable and respectable life as a math teacher, another staff member from Jews for Jesus passed through the area. We met and he urged me to consider investing my life as an evangelist. I knew how difficult it had been for me to consider Jesus. Here was an opportunity to spend my life speaking to my own people about a matter of life and death. For the first time, I said I would talk to God about it.

A couple of months passed and I could not shake the idea. Moishe's question was still hanging in the air. I called San Francisco to talk to him. A few months later, in September 1979, Patty and I joined the staff of Jews for Jesus. We've lived in San Francisco, Chicago, Washington, D.C., New York . . . and in 1998 we packed up and moved with our three children to Sydney, Australia. When you hand over the reins of your life to God you never know where you will end up—but it's always an adventure!

By way of a postscript, a few words about my Grandma Bessie. She never wanted to have anything to do with the person of Jesus for as long as I could remember. Whenever I would try to broach the subject, she would flick the back of her hand in the air to indicate her disinterest. She refused even to pronounce the name "Jesus." It was a painful memory to her and so many of our people who sustained hurt, humiliation, rejection and even death from those who named Jesus as their God and motivator.

When Grandma was put in a nursing care facility it had nothing to do with her wits, but rather the frailty of her aging body. One October morning, I went there for an early visit. Rarely would I bring my Bible to visit her because she had made it so clear, so often, that she was not interested in hearing anything from the Bible. Nevertheless, I brought it in that day.

I began speaking to the charge nurse assigned to Grandma Bessie's floor. She wanted to know what I did for a living and I told her I worked with Jews for Jesus. She was thrilled, since she, too, was a believer in Jesus. We spoke about eternal things as I approached Grandma's room.

As soon as I walked in the door, Grandma greeted me with, "What was it you were talking about just now?"

Matter-of-factly I answered, "We were talking about the forgiveness of sins that Jesus offers and the eternal life that he brings."

"I would like to hear more about that," she announced. My jaw nearly hit the ground! With surprise and delight, I opened the Bible and began reading to her. I could almost see something going on in her heart and mind as she listened. After 30 minutes of conversation, I asked Grandma, "Would you like to accept God's forgiveness through Jesus now?" And at the age of 96, she did!

The peace and joy that flooded her soul were evident. Her eyes lit up and her face shone. She continued to shine for five more years, until at the age of 101, she left this earth and went to meet her Messiah face to face.

If you want to know the truth about Jesus, it doesn't matter if you are young, old or in-between. Please ask God to tell you what is real. If you think it might help to talk to another Jew who believes in Jesus, I hope you will contact us.

Bob Mendelsohn
P.O. Box 925
Sydney, NSW 2001
AUSTRALIA
jewsforjesus.org.au

JEWS F✡R JESUS®
International Headquarters
60 Haight Street
San Francisco, CA 94102
U.S.A.
www.jewsforjesus.org

Since 1999, when this booklet was first published, Bob continues to write updates, blogs and tweets regularly. His stories and teachings are also included as well as text, video and podcast/audio sermons. These are all available on the Australian Jews for Jesus website: jewsforjesus.org.au

GLOSSARY

Baal teshuvah: In the past, this phrase was used to describe one who turned away from Judaism, but later returned to embrace it. Now it is more commonly used to refer to any Jewish person who decides to move from a less religious or non–religious lifestyle to one of observing Orthodox Jewish laws and rituals.

Bar mitzvah: Literally "son of the commandment." This rite of passage at age thirteen marks the entrance of a Jewish boy into the Jewish religious community (which for traditional Jews includes observance of the commandments of the Torah). It includes a public reading from the Torah and is often followed by an elaborate celebration.

Bimah: The synagogue platform from which the Torah is read.

Bubbe: Grandmother.

Daven: Means "to pray" in Yiddish. Refers to reciting Jewish prayers, often with a rocking motion. (past tense = "davened")

Frum: Very religious, observant of Jewish law.

Haggadah: Literally, "the narrative" or "story." This is the book (or in some cases, condensed booklet) which gives the order of service for the Passover celebration. The Haggadah tells the story of how God brought Israel out from slavery in Egypt. It includes narratives, songs, psalms and other prayers to commemorate freedom and praise the Almighty for his mighty acts of redemption.

Kavanah: Intention, devotion. Refers to a sense of spirituality that is supposed to breathe life into ritual.

Ma'ariv: Evening prayers. The daily service recited at night after sunset.

Minchah: Afternoon prayers. The second service of the day, recited in the afternoon up to sunset.

Mitzvot: plural of mitzvah: command, observance, good deed. A mitzvah may refer to one of the 613 commandments, or it may simply refer to any act of kindness.

Musaf: Additional prayers recited on Sabbath, Holidays and Rosh Chodesh (New Moon).

Ruach: Spirit.

Shah!: "Shhhh!" or "Quiet!"

Shabbes goy: A non-Jew employed by a religious Jew to perform tasks on the Sabbath that are prohibited on that day by traditional religious practice—such as turning lights on and off.

Shacharit: Morning prayers. The first service of the day. Its name is derived from the Hebrew word shachar, meaning "dawn" or "daybreak."

Sh'ma: Passage of Scripture from Deuteronomy 6:4–9. It is chanted as one of the most important of all Jewish prayers and affirms the sovereignty and oneness of God. The recitation in the synagogue also includes Deuteronomy 11:13–21, 15:37–41.

Shul: Synagogue.

Tefillin: Small leather boxes to be strapped on the arm and forehead for prayer, in which are encased Scriptures inscribed on parchment. Two of the Scriptures are from Exodus (13:1–10 and 13:11–16) and the other two are from Deuteronomy (6:4–9 and 11:13–21). The ritual of strapping the tefillin on for prayer is referred to as "laying tefillin," or "putting on tefillin." It is done in accordance with the traditional understanding of Exodus 13:9, "And it shall be for a sign upon thy hand and for a frontlet between thine eyes." The ritual is to be performed by the men each morning, except for Sabbaths and holidays.

If you would like to read other stories of Jews who are for Jesus, check out the Jews for Jesus web site on page 26.

Look for titles such as:

Books:
- *Stories of Jews for Jesus*, Ruth Rosen, Editor
- *Jewish Doctors Meet the Great Physician*, Ruth Rosen, Editor
- *The Last Jew of Rotterdam*, Ernest Cassutto
- *Between Two Fathers*, Charles Barg, M.D.
- *Bound for the Promised Land*, Haya Benhayim with Menahem Benhayim

Booklets:
- *Drawn to Jesus: The Journey of a Jewish Artist*, David Rothstein
- *Loss to Life*, Susan Perlman
- *Nothing to Fear*, Karol Joseph
- *Hineni: Here Am I, But Where Are You?* Tuvya Zaretsky
- *From Generation to Generation*, Steve Wertheim

DVDs:
- *Survivor Stories: Finding Hope from an Unlikely Source*
- *Forbidden Peace: The Story Behind the Headlines*
- *Flowers of the Son*